A Spiritual Guide to the Scientific 21st Century

A Spiritual Guide to the Scientific 21st Century

Gerhard C. F. Miller

VANTAGE PRESS
New York

"Time Exposures" and "Eye of God" are used with the permission of *National Geographic*. "Science and God: A Warming Trend?" reprinted with permission from the American Association for the Advancement of Science. Copyright 1998 American Association for the Advancement of Science.

FIRST EDITION

All rights reserved, including the right of
reproduction in whole or in part in any form.

Copyright © 2000 by Gerhard C. F. Miller

Published by Vantage Press, Inc.
516 West 34th Street, New York, New York 10001

Manufactured in the United States of America
ISBN: 0-533-13029-8

Library of Congress Catalog Card No.: 98-91052

0 9 8 7 6 5 4 3 2

To my wife Ruth, my parents,
and a loss of a dear friend.

Poetry is simply the most beautiful, impressive, and widely effective mode of saying things.
—Matthew Arnold

I consider poetry the warp that binds together the beauty of literature.
—Gerhard C. F. Miller

Contents

Foreword	xi
Acknowledgments	xiii
Author's Note	xv
Introduction	1
Supreme Intelligence	50
Supreme Energy	52
Supreme Love	55
Faith	59
Prayer	63
Conclusion	69
Bibliography	77

Foreword

During one's lifetime, the physical and mechanical body functions in harmony with the universe. However, the other part, the human psyche—the soul—occupies no space, but is our link with eternity. The soul is one's compass that silently and surely keeps us on course for our journey on earth. We know where the mind and body go when the life span ends, but perhaps you have wondered what becomes of the soul.

Science will continue to produce many miracles that will benefit everyone. By combining what modern science reveals to us about the universe with the age-old beliefs about reincarnation, we can gain new confidence in the teachings about everlasting life.

It is hoped that what you read in these pages will expand your thinking in such a way that you will find it natural to adapt to the new twenty-first century.

And as your thinking expands, so will your appreciation of the awesome wonders and splendor of the universe that surrounds you and of which your Creator has made you a part. This is the place to insert remarks by a dear friend of mine.

"God is nature; nature is God. This world is my heaven. Artists are my angels. Their creations are prayers and songs of praise, appreciation and wonderment.

"Every cloud, every sunflower and every rose, every redwood and chestnut tree, every indigo bunting and hummingbird is a miracle to me. The sun, the moon, northern lights, thunder and lightning, rain showers and snowstorms, hurricanes and tornadoes are spectacular mysteries and messages to me.

"The immense star-spangled universe above, below, all around this planet is incomprehensible to me. Since my mind cannot comprehend the incomprehensible, this beautiful earth with all its natural glories around me will be my Heaven for the rest of my days.

"Enjoy—please enjoy it every day. It will enrich your life and soothe your soul.

"For now it is all we have."

>
> Frank J. Pechman
> (Remarks at the 1991 Opening Exhibition
> of James Ingwersen's paintings at the
> Miller Art Museum)

Acknowledgments

My very special thanks first go to my wife, Ruth, who has been such a help. Both in writing and painting one often gets so involved in concentration that essential details get overlooked. Ruth has the ability to spot them, for which I am thankful.

My thanks also go to thoughtful friends—among them Carl Scholz, Elizabeth Parsons, Dr. Roberta Nauman, Frank Pechman, Richard Follmer, Patricia Boldt, and Sharon Kamada. Also I am grateful to my cousin, Dr. Raymond Miller, a specialist in the field of computer science as well as the science of advanced mathematics. Again, my thanks to Alice Sautebin who has been so patient about keeping me on friendly terms with her computer.

Author's Note

The subject of this book could be complex and lengthy; however, it has been purposely planned to be short and easily understood.

It does, however, require an open mind that is free from prejudice. I suggest that the reader set aside time to read this book in a location that is quiet, comfortable, and free from distractions. Then, later, continue with casual reading. As a result of our scientific thinking skills, the next century will be vastly different from those of the past. This text offers insights into the probable salient aspects of the twenty-first century.

It is my hope that by adjusting to the Scientific Age, Christianity will manage to survive.

Introduction

People have been searching for a higher power since the beginning of time—an outside strength to turn to in times of need. Primitive people found special comfort in the belief that somewhere "out there" was a God-empowered Spirit, or idol (sometimes in one's image) that had the miraculous ability to control what happened to their personal lives in this world.

Years ago I attended a lecture by Marcus Bach, author of the book, *If You Had Been Born into Another Faith*. While it dealt with many of the various religions and codes of ethics found around the world, its main direction was focused on the "good" to be found in each of them. The Golden Rule can be considered the *red thread* that binds all great religions together: "Do unto others as you would have them do unto you."

Some years ago we experienced an example of the good that is a part of every religion.

Chichicastenango is a town in the highlands of Guatemala that is built around a large market square. On the east side stands a large Roman Catholic cathedral, and facing it across the square is the temple of the witch doctor. In our travels to paint and write, my wife, Ruth, and I were fortunate to have spent some time there. We were surprised to learn that its citizens were enough removed from present-day civilization that they could worship a Christian God and the gods of their native ancestors at the same time.

In the spring, before planting time, the Indians bring seeds of the various crops that they intend to plant, mainly corn and beans, to the cathedral. After the seeds are arranged in neat piles down the long central aisle of the church, the priest walks down the aisle to bless and sprinkle the seeds with holy water to insure a good crop.

Outside on the broad steps, the Indians carry on a ceremony of their own by swinging their smoking copal-burning *incenscerios*. This is followed by firing off large, homemade sky rockets to get their prayers up to heaven.

Next, a parade is organized to march around the square to the temple of the witch doctor.

The Indians, who have been told by the priest about the suffering and crucifixion of Christ, also have been told to follow his example and emulate him. This they do in a strange way, by drinking a powerful liquor called *aguadiente*. In this way they believe, in their own way, that they can experience the suffering of the Christ.

Finally, the procession arrives in front of the temple of the witch doctor. **Those not too inebriated to climb the steps to the portico of the temple then reverently genuflect in each of the four directions of the compass and ask "*El dio* *del mundo*" (God of the world) to bless everyone in the world.

From there, anyone who has a special request to ask of the witch doctor is led up the hill to the shrine where the idol—the earthly representative of *El dio del mundo*—is located, and where the witch doctor will intercede to bring about the fulfillment of a personal request.

One day, when I was having a visit with the priest, I was informed that the success or failure of his mission depended on his ability to compromise with the ancient beliefs.

This serves as an example of the pre-Christian way of thinking that still exists in some parts of the world.

About two thousand years ago, Christ, the world's greatest reformer, announced a revolutionary new discovery when he said, "The Father and I are one"; and, "he that has seen me has seen the Father."

Roughly two thousand years after that, Albert Einstein, one of the world's greatest scientists, announced another revolutionary discovery when he introduced the world to his "Quantum Theory" and the "Theory of Relativity." In this way he transformed thinking in a way that now makes all of us at one with the universe and its Creator.

Fifty years ago, not long after Einstein made his

announcement, I published Residue, a book of poetry, in which the following poem appeared:

> Gather me up from out the corners
> of Thy universe, O God,
> that while I live,
> though I am not to know my days,
> impart to me
> the energy
> of yon distant glowing star,
> whose tremulous music from afar
> resounds through harp strings of tall pine
> to focus on this heart of mine
> where cosmic forces concentrate
> to be set free.
>
> Gather me up from sunshine, air and food,
> for I am not sustained by self;
> a pensioner of the universe,
> powerless of my own accord
> but setting free
> what Thou hast gathered up in me.

This was one of a series of poems written at a time in my life that was richly blessed by an accumulation of inspiring events.

Though I did not realize it at the time, this poem sets the stage for a completely new way of thinking as it leads into the scientific age that we now realize we have grown into—an age in which thinking humans find the old paradigms do not satisfy.

Too often, the old, fixed beliefs block the acquisition of important new knowledge.

My work in the middle 1940s kept me busy in town all day long and often my wife would plan her shopping time for late in the day so I could ride home with her after work. However, when the days grew shorter in the fall, I often preferred to walk the three miles home, especially on a night lit by the radiance of a full moon.

The walk took about an hour. This would be just enough time to become thoroughly saturated with the wonders of the universe, and to absorb the energy for the production of inspired poetry.

At this point I would like to tell a story told to me by a very dear friend:

Olga was five years old at the end of the nineteenth century. She was put to bed and told by her grandfather that she would be awakened and dressed before midnight, as there was something he wanted her to see. When the clock struck twelve, her grandfather took her out onto the front porch.

"Look, Olenka," (Olenka being Little Olga in Bohemian) he said, "this is the beginning of a new century. And just like the fresh snow on the lawn, there isn't a mark on it. But it will be a great new century because wonderful things are going to happen. There is a man in Italy who has discovered how to pick sound out of the air. There is a man in Detroit who has invented a machine that will go without being drawn by horses. And there are two brothers in the East who have invented a machine that will fly like a bird. You will see all of these things, but I will not."

Years later, Olga flew from Los Angeles to Europe via the North Pole route.

My wife, Ruth, and I came onto the scene at the beginning of this twentieth century (she in 1902 and I in 1903). Now, as we are closing in on the end of this century and look back, it seems to become sort of a "good news—bad news" chronicle that includes many marvelous things. We have lived through two world wars, which were fought to make the world safe for democracy, a Korean conflict, a Vietnamese conflict, and smaller brushfire conflicts so numerous that we have hardly been able to inhale a peaceful breath between them.

In the eighteenth century, for example, when people's minds were fixed in time, they took for granted that things would always be "this way."

At the time of Thomas Jefferson's inaugural, Henry Adams wrote: "Great as were the material obstacles in the path of the United States, the greatest obstacle of all was in the human mind. Down to the close of the eighteenth century, no changes had occurred in the world which warranted practical men in assuming that great changes were to come."

But the good news includes, for example, scientific progress that has gone ahead by leaps and bounds. However, evolution in religious thinking has lagged far behind. As you will discover a little later, some of the eighteenth century "minds fixed in time" that Henry Adams referred to, have continued into the twentieth century and will, doubtless, be found well into the twenty-first.

I was born on my father's twenty-eighth birthday. He came onto the scene near the end of the nineteenth century. His father, the Rev. Fredrick Miller, was a dedicated Lutheran pastor. I remember his library. It was a small room. Stacked on shelves on three sides, from floor to ceiling, were books on theology—all in German, and most leatherbound and very old. In fact, he had one book that was written by the man who preached Martin Luther's funeral sermon.

My grandfather served a parish in Amelith, Michigan, as well as another parish about seven miles away. In Amelith, the family lived in a log cabin built in 1855. He served this congregation from 1867 until 1899. During his time of service of 31 years, the congregation doubled in size. Later he was a pastor and parochial school teacher in Shelby, Michigan until his retirement nineteen years later. My grandmother would supply him with six hard-boiled eggs to fuel him for the long horseback ride from one to the other. These, he said, stuck to his ribs better.

In those early days, a pastor's salary consisted

mainly of donations of chickens and eggs, plus, from time to time, a quarter of beef or pork. The collection plate supplied whatever cash could be garnered.

So, with three of my father's brothers in college and seminary planning to follow in their father's footsteps, it became my father's lot, as number seven in a family of twelve, to go to work at age ten after having completed his education consisting of four years in a German parochial school.

He got a job driving a team of horses and hauling soil out of the large irrigation ditches being constructed near Saginaw, Michigan. This was hard work for a small boy, so he quit and got a job working for a Jewish clothing merchant in Saginaw. He was fourteen at the time. His pay was five dollars a week, but he couldn't get board and room for less then seven dollars a week, so he stayed at home near Bay City and rode his bicycle the five miles back and forth to work every day. It was there in the store that he learned to speak English from a Greek who wanted to learn German.

He became skilled as a window-trimmer. It was at a time when the fashion was to enhance the window displays with a great variety of puffed-up crepe and tissue paper.

Mr. Greisen, a store owner in Wisconsin, read an article written by my father that was published in a national window-trimming magazine. He wrote to Dad, offering a job for the summer months. Dad accepted, and when my grandmother heard about it, she was so upset she had my grandfather go to the store in Saginaw to talk him out of going. She had heard horror stories about Indian atrocities in that area. Grandfather was not having much luck talking Father out of going. Finally he asked, "Did you tell Mr. Greisen you would take the job?"

"Yes," Dad said, "I did."

"Well then, you will have to go," Grandfather replied.

So it was that on a miserable, cold, rainy night in May, he got off a boat in the strange little town of Sturgeon Bay, Wisconsin. This was in 1896. He was twenty-one years old at the time.

He worked for Mr. Greisen for two years and in the Washburn department store for another two years. His plans were to open a men's clothing store of his own, so in preparation, he spent three months in a "business school" in Milwaukee where he learned the principles of double-entry bookkeeping.

He saved his money religiously and in 1901 opened his own store with a capital start-up fund of $600. He was engaged to be married at the time, but this had to be temporarily postponed as he had promised his mother he would never marry until he had saved $100. Business was good, so he and my mother were married in 1902. The end of the nineteenth century and the beginning of the twentieth was a red letter time in his life.

With a heritage of many Lutheran pastors going way back in his family, and with Father's grandfather coming to America as a missionary to the poor unchurched in this land, it was only natural that his church affiliations should be with a Lutheran church.

As a youngster I sat Sunday after Sunday listening to long German services and not understanding more than *"Unser vater vor bist am himmel* (Our Father who art in heaven)." However, when it came time for confirmation instructions, we got them in English.

This was not long after the turn of the century when the main purpose of religious teaching was to spread the doctrine of hellfire and damnation—hook, line, and sinker. We were taught that unless we went to communion five times a year we would go straight to hell, and the same fate awaited those who had not been baptized. Sad to say, in some churches the same archaic teachings from the dark ages still persist.

My brother and I were growing up and beginning to do some independent thinking. We wanted to know why we couldn't listen to English and not always German. Father agreed with us.

It was then we discovered how politics enters into religion and what a good politician our German pastor was. He would come to Father and say, "There are some of the young people who want English services and, if you agree with them, when we have the annual meeting, you will have to stand up and vote that way."

Then he would go to some of his die-hard German members and say, "There are some of the young people who want English services and if you want to continue all German services you will have to vote that way."

Then came time for the annual meeting, with the pastor conducting the business. Finally the question came up: "Should we have two English and two German services a month?" Both men and women stood up to vote, and he counted the men, but not the women. Then the next question: "Should we continue with all-German services?" Again both men and women stood up, but this time he counted both men and women.

Knowing that then, and even today, the women were not allowed to vote in our church, I jumped to my feet. "You miscounted the vote," I said.

"Don't you think I know how to count, young man?" he asked.

"You counted the men and women one time, but not the other," I said.

"Sit down!" he ordered.

"I won't sit down," I said. "You are conducting a crooked voting procedure."

"Young man," he said, "I want you to come up in front of the congregation and apologize to me."

"I don't have to apologize to a crook," I said and I

turned around and walked out of the church, leaving my embarrassed mother and father sitting there.

Later Dad complimented me for standing up to the pastor. I know, if he had been me, he would have done the same thing. It did not take them long to find another church affiliation.

Sadly enough, unless one has the fortitude to stand up for what is right, the old taboos will persist.

The short view is that "history repeats itself"; the long view, fortunately, is that the evolutionary flow of the cosmos brings constant change, with each age revealing something that has not been known before.

In the field of science, one of the most renowned thinkers has been Albert Einstein, who has opened our eyes to the mysteries of the universe. When he was asked, "Is there a reality outside us?," he answered, "Yes, I believe there is." He believed that with the exploration of this reality outside us, a new era would begin for humanity.

When Einstein was asked what he thought about during some of his long periods of contemplation, he said, "I want to know God's thoughts! The rest are details."

Others of his famous quotes: "Only a life lived for others is a life worthwhile." Also, "The moral urge is the most valuable traditional endowment of humanity." [*Albert Einstein—The Human Side,* by Helen Dukas and Banesh Hoffmann]

Einstein went only so far as to call his "Quantum Theory" and his "Theory of Relativity" *theories,* as he always left room for something beyond.

Another outstanding leader guiding us into the twenty-first century is the Indian M.D., Deepak Chopra. A number of his books have become bestsellers, i.e., *Timeless Mind and Ageless Body, Perfect Health* and an important daily text on the *Seven Spiritual Laws of Success.* His way of channeling thought into the "quantum" universe makes one feel totally at home with all of nature and the Creator.

Dr. Chopra has the advantage of combining the medical knowledge of both the Occident and the Orient. He is rethinking medicine in a holistic way that involves both the mind and body. The science of medicine has made great strides, and now, with his "Ayurvedic" approach (see his book, *Timeless Mind and Ageless Body*), he has made an even greater leap forward. Thinking in new ways and medical research will extend the useful life of humans as we learn more about our mechanical bodies and how to care for them.

A recent comment by a reader of *Time* magazine reads: "Bravo for your article explaining the role of spirituality in healing.

"For thousands of years, mystics have been saying the mind and body are one. Doctors can surgically remove the symptoms of illness, but if it remains in the mind, it will return to the body. According to Chopra, the whole system needs to be treated. I hope that more of the medical community will take the opportunity to bridge the mind-body connection, looking to Chopra as the leader and the spokesman helping to bring medicine and mysticism closer together." (Medicine 6–24–96)

Gradually, both scientific and religious leaders are pointing with hope toward an enlightened new century.

I have recently received a "News and Comment" clipping that appeared in *Science*—a magazine published by the American Association for the Advancement of Science. The contents of this article are so in harmony with what I have written, up to this point, that parts of it require quoting word for word.

Science and God: A Warming Trend?

Can rational inquiry and spiritual conviction be reconciled? Although some scientists contend that the two cannot coexist, others believe they have linked destinies.

"Keep that which is committed to thy trust, avoiding profane and vain babblings and oppositions of science falsely so called," the New Testament cautions in one of the Bible's rare references to science (1 Timothy 6:20, King James translation) This verse helped set the tone for 2000 years of antagonism between scientific inquiry and spiritual conviction—a history of strife stretching from the religious persecution of Baruch Spinoza and Galileo Galilei through the 1860 boast by the biologist Thomas Huxley, the first popularizer of Darwinism, that "extinguished theologians lie about the cradle of every science, as strangled snakes beside that of Hercules."

Maybe it's the greenhouse effect, but recent signs point toward a thaw in the ice between science and faith. In the religion camp, the Vatican has at last formally apologized for its arrest of Galileo, while recently Pope John Paul II gingerly acknowledged evolution to be "more than just a hypothesis." Later this year, the Fuller Theological Seminary in Pasadena, California, the intellectual hub of conservative Protestant denominations, will publish a book acknowledging a natural origin for the human family tree. And increasingly, spiritual thinkers are endorsing the proposition of German theologian Dietrich Bonhoeffer, who wrote in the early 1940s that growing understanding of the natural world simply means people need no longer look to the church for answers to questions they can now answer for themselves.

On the research side, both the National Academy of Sciences and the American Association for the Advancement of Science (AAAS, which publishes this magazine) have launched projects to promote a dialogue between science and religion. New institutions aimed at bridging the gap have been formed, including the Chicago Center for Religion and Science, and the Center for Theology and Natural Sciences in Berkeley, California. Universities such as Cambridge and Princeton also have established professorships or lectureships on the reconciliation of the two camps.

Another sign of easing tensions is scientists' increasing willingness to discuss their spiritual beliefs in public. Nobel Prize winner Charles Townes (see article following) devoted 30 pages to religious questions in his 1995 book on physics, *Making Waves*. Sir John Houghton, former head of the scientists' working group of the Intergovernmental Panel on Climate Change, is a devout believer who in 1994 published a book on global warming not with a university press, but a religious house. Houghton recently discussed his faith during a speech at a scientific meeting, and says "I expected to be attacked, but the reception was warm, which might not have happened a few years ago." God talk has come into vogue among some scientists, with theoretical physicist Stephen Hawking of Cambridge University writing that big-bang cosmology may reveal "the mind of God," and astrophysicist George Smoot of Lawrence Berkeley National Laboratory in California suggesting that background radiation represents "the handwriting of God." Strikingly, a 1997 poll by Edward Larson of the University of Georgia, Athens, published in *Nature,* has found that about 40% of working physicists and biologists hold strong spiritual beliefs.

. . . mainstream faith must show it can accommodate scientific thought.

. . . Francis Collins, [a geneticist and director of the National Human Genome Research Institute at the National Institutes of Health] who co-directed the team that found the gene for cystic fibrosis, has worked in an African missionary hospital and de-

Look up - Oh man

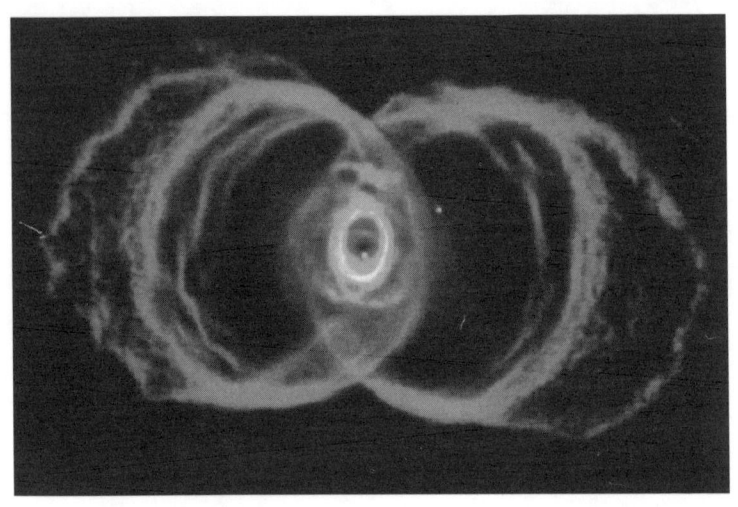

The Eye of God—Hubble Telescope, 1997.

THE HUBBLE
TELESCOPE
VIEWS THE
UNIVERSE
FROM SPACE

Time
Exposures

By WILLIAM R. NEWCOTT
NATIONAL GEOGRAPHIC EDITORIAL STAFF

Astronomers looked 8,000 light-years into the cosmos with the Hubble Space Telescope, and it seemed that the eye of God was staring back. The Etched Hourglass Nebula is actually a shell of gas expanding from a dying star. In the Helix Nebula (below) a dying star creates knots of gas and dust twice the diameter of our solar system. Once a rare sight, thousands of such knots—and myriad other cosmic surprises—are now seen through Hubble's unmatched eye.

RAGHVENDRA SAHAI, JOHN TRAUGER, AND NASA (LEFT); ROBERT O'DELL, KENNY HANDRON, AND NASA

scribes himself as a "serious" Christian. He does not hesitate to find religious implications in his work. "When something new is revealed about the human genome," Collins says, "I experience a feeling of awe at the realization that humanity now knows something only God knew before. It is a deeply moving sensation that helps me appreciate the spiritual side of life, and also makes the practice of science more rewarding. A lot of scientists really don't know what they are missing by not exploring their spiritual feelings."

... David Scott, a former Berkeley physicist who is now chancellor of the University of Massachusetts, Amherst, says, "Yet the truly great scientists were not afraid to ponder larger religious aspects of their work. They found this intellectually engaging," Scott notes. Newton, for instance, was fascinated by biblical prophecy. He argued that the more-or-less uniform zodiac of the planets did not occur by chance and showed an aesthetic sense on the part of a Maker. Werner Heisenberg drew on Eastern mysticism to help develop uncertainty theory.

... Joshua Lederberg, an evolutionary biologist at Rockefeller University in New York City and 1958 Nobel winner, says, "Nothing so far disproves the divine. What is incontrovertible is that a religious impulse guides our motive in sustaining scientific inquiry. Beyond that, it's all speculation."

... Reverend Christopher Carlisle, a chaplain for the University of Massachusetts, Amherst, adds that it is not at all clear that rational inquiry is capable of detecting larger purpose to the universe: "The lab only measures what's in the lab. It is tautological to say that you do not find the divine when you test for the physical." He cites as an example the spiritual paradox that the more you give of yourself the more you gain. "What laboratory test could detect that? Yet I can show you human beings where the effect is unquestionably present and acutely moving."

Some contemporary believers even argue that scientific advances might be seen as dovetailing with biblical accounts. When astrophysicist and Catholic abbe Georges Lemaitre first proposed in 1927 that the universe began with the detonation of a "primordial atom," the idea later dubbed the big bang, many scientists opposed the theory in part because it seemed overly reminiscent of the Genesis story of a discrete moment of creation. In addition, the troubling enigma of what might have sparked the big bang seemed to fit right in with Aristotle's contention that temporal existence was set in motion by a supernatural "unmoved mover." Today, some theologians are warming to the big-bang theory as they become aware of its spiritual parallels.

... The case for a Maker is further strengthened, in the eyes of some researchers, by the fact that science has not yet accounted for the origin of life. Evolutionary biology can explain adaptation and descent, notes Belgium's de Duve, but so far there's no scientific consensus on how natural selection and other living processes began in the first place. Until such time as biologists can demonstrate an entirely material origin for life, the divine will remain a contender. "I am unaware of any irreconcilable conflict between scientific knowledge about evolution and the idea of a creator God," Collins says. "Why couldn't God have used the mechanism of evolution to create?"

... The Society of Ordained Scientists' Peacocke sees it similarly: "Science and religion are the intellectual forces that do not reject the dreams of the Enlightenment and do not think all ideas reduce to nihility under a social contextual critique. Long after post-modern intellectual fads have exhausted themselves, science and religion will still be here and still be searching."

Perhaps the fact that the two schools of thought have so often been at each other's throats stems from mutual recognition of their linked destinies, and their joint commitment to the idea that the truth is out there. Rather than being driven ever farther apart, tomorrow's scientist and theologian may seek each other's solace.

—Gregg Easterbrook
(*Science*; Vol. 277, 15 August 1997; www.sciencemag.org)

Of Lasers and Prayer

"It is not uncommon for good scientists to be believers," says a scientist clearly in the "good" category, physicist Charles Townes, who in 1964 shared with two Russian researchers the Nobel Prize for the invention of the laser. Townes, who has also been provost of the Massachusetts Institute of Technology, is a lifelong churchgoer and a devout, although "non-doctrinaire," believer. He prays daily and "accepts the Bible as a record of history" one with "no strong conflict with contemporary science, unless you insist on taking Scripture literally."

Born in Greenville, South Carolina, Townes graduated from the California Institute of Technology in 1939 and went to work for Bell Laboratories just as the lab was shifting its focus from research to applied engineering for World War II. Assigned to a hush-hush project to develop combat radar, Townes irked superiors by suggesting that the wavelength they had chosen would be absorbed by water vapor, neutralizing the device in the humid air of the Pacific theater. He turned out to be right, and the early American combat radars for World War II were of limited value. "This got me thinking about the relationship between microwaves and molecules, a field that was practically nonexistent," Townes says.

After the war, Townes began to explore microwave spectroscopy, aided by a storage room stuffed with equipment from failed radar projects. Eventually he realized that tightly controlled microwaves could be produced by stimulating molecules, such as ammonia, which led to his discovery of the maser. (As a result of this discovery, a device for (M) microwave (A) amplification by (S) stimulated (E) emission of (R) radiation has made it possible for a microwave oven to become a common household appliance.) Townes and a Bell colleague, Arthur Schawlow, then applied the same principle to light and won the first U.S. patents on the laser. Townes says God was a "source of strength" during these historic discoveries, aiding him at times to overcome self-doubt. Later Townes delved into radio and infrared astronomy, helping establish that organic compounds are present in large volumes in space. In 1981, he chaired the commission that persuaded President Reagan not to field large numbers of the highly destructive MX missile. Townes says that before each commission meeting, he prayed for guidance. Today, at 82, Townes is a University Professor emeritus at the University of California, Berkeley, and continues to supervise astronomy graduate students.

Townes does not see science and faith as opposing forces. "Science wants to know the mechanism of the universe, religion the meaning. The two cannot be separated," he says. "Many scientists feel there is no place in research for discussion of anything that sounds mystical. But it is unreasonable to think we already know enough about the natural world to be confident about the totality of forces. That is more illogical than any claim of illogic made against faith."

Townes believes science and religion are about to enter a cycle of reconciliation, as researchers find themselves up against seemingly unanswerable questions, among them what triggered the big bang and why, of many possible outcomes, quantum cosmology seems to favor those circumstances that lead to a stable universe. "Physicists are running into stone walls of things that seem to reflect intelligence at work in natural law," he asserts. "Biologists (also) will hit stone walls if they fail to find explanations for essential effects like sudden jumps in neurological sophistication."

Townes even uses the unfashionable term "design," despite the main current of 20th century thought, which views life and the universe as existing independently of any divine influence. "The more we know about the cosmos and evolutionary biology, the more they seem inexplicable without some aspect of [intelligent] design," Townes asserts. "And for me that inspires faith."—G.E. (*Science*; vol. 277, 15 August 1997; www.sciencemag.org)

Recently, the Rev. Robert Schuller made the statement that science and religion are opposite sides of the same coin. He quotes Psalm 18:28: "For you will light my lamp: the Lord my God will enlighten my darkness." To quote him further: "Scientific inquiry has found tremendous support from the Christian religion. Our compassion for suffering souls has motivated Christians to support research into the causes for many major diseases. True religion is the pursuit of truth, for real truth liberates. Positive religion educates and education sets people free from ignorance, superstition and prejudice. People of faith never fear truth. No wonder so many brilliant scientists are positive believers."

James Redfield in his book, *The Celestine Prophecy,* quotes one of his characters as saying, "People should come to religion because of love, not out of fear." How refreshing this is in the light of much of what was taught at the beginning of the twentieth century.

The church, which had a small but vital beginning, has had a fragmented growth, which, in a perfectly evolutionary way, kept it strong and from becoming ingrown.

As with everything that exists in the universe, religion is slowly evolving into a more comfortable existence with itself. As ecumenism is taking over, intolerance and bigotry are being squeezed out. In some parts of the country groups of young people, especially college students, are meeting in small groups for the purpose of religious study. They are being stimulated and excited by many of the fine books being written and published. They are the best hope for our new century.

Looking far into the future, as Isaiah did long before the birth of Christ, the day will come when "the earth shall be full of the knowledge of the Lord as the waters cover the sea." (Isaiah 11:9 RSV)

Evolution can be considered the Creator's timetable . It began before the universe was formed and will continue on into infinity. In the course of history, timing is of paramount importance.

THE FIRST REFORMATION was begun by a brave young Jew by the name of Jesus. He so violently protested against the abuses that had corrupted the religion of his day that he suffered crucifixion at the hands of his own people.

THE SECOND REFORMATION was slow in coming. It began with Piere Waldo, a merchant in Lyon, France, in about 1110. However, this reformation did not generate full momentum until the sixteenth century. It had, for its object, the reform of the Western Roman Catholic Church that led to the establishment of Protestant churches.

John Hus (1369–1415), a professor at the university in Prague, had been ordered by the church to attend a conference in Constance. He had been guaranteed safe conduct. But upon his arrival, he was placed under house arrest for over a year. In the end he was tried and found guilty of treason against the church and was burned at the stake.

Martin Luther (1483–1546), a priest of the Augustana order, also protested against the Roman Catholic evil practice of selling indulgences. This was supposed to make it possible to buy one's way out of purgatory for a price. Luther, in protest, nailed his Ninety-five Theses on the door of the church in Wittenberg. The church could not tolerate this behavior and he was ordered to be tried at a Diet in Worms. When being forced to recant, he refused. Fortunately, he had influential friends in high places who pretended to capture him and spirit him away to Wartburg Castle where he was protected from the church. It was there that he translated the New Testament from Latin into German. Luther was a hardworking clergyman and also a good friend of the Count of Saxe-Coburg. It was there in the mighty Coburg Castle that he composed his famous hymn, "Ein Feste Burg ist Unser Gott."

THE THIRD REFORMATION, which has also been slow in coming, has been with us for some time. However, with the scientific age that has taken on explosive force, we need to rethink our lives. Those human beings who are not stuck in time, are finding that the old paradigms do not satisfy, and that a new and bright spiritual life can replace the archaic dictates they have listened to for years. Thus, the beauty and majesty of the universe that surround us, and of which we are all a part, will give new excitement to life. It will take time, but reformations always do.

It makes no difference whatever the time in history, authority does not like to be challenged. That is exactly the problem Christ faced; I am not surprised that he was crucified. What really surprises me is that those in authority did not carry out their threats sooner.

When in a rage, Christ went into the temple where he tipped over the tables of the moneychangers, drove out those who sold doves and animals for sacrifice, and accused them of desecrating the house of God by turning it into a den of thieves. Imagine how that angered those in authority at that time!

Naturally those in authority were out to trap him by accusing him of associating with sinners and prostitutes. And Christ, when he caught them about to enforce the Jewish law by stoning a poor girl accused of prostitution, turned to them and in an accusing voice said, "Whoever of you is without sin, cast the first stone." Then they all, one by one, turned and walked away and plotted how they could get rid of this troublemaker.

Everywhere Jesus went he attracted large

crowds. This was not surprising. He performed miracles that endeared him to everyone, except the priests and Pharisees, who were losing their followers to this upstart, who accused them of being hypocrites and vipers. He healed the sick, restored sight to the blind, cleansed the lepers, and did things they could not do.

In the light of what the twenty-first century might reveal about the earthly life of Christ, the great reformer, we would do well to look back about two thousand years to his origin and his life.

I can imagine God saying: "I am going to create a creature above all others on my earth. He will be called Jesus, the Savior. I will father him by my Spirit, but he will be born as a man."

Again I can imagine God saying: "I will guide his every step through his life, and protect him so that in all things he will do my will. That is my reason for creating him."

So when Jesus was an infant, God did protect him by having Mary and Joseph take him to Egypt out of the reach of the jealous wrath of Herod.

When Jesus was probably about twelve years old, he went with his mother and Joseph, who were devout Jews, to celebrate the Passover in Jerusalem. It was not until they were almost home in Nazareth that they missed him. They made the long trip back to Jerusalem, and after searching for three days, found him in the temple in deep discussion with some of the most learned teachers of the land who were astounded at the wisdom of this young lad.

Mary scolded him: "Why have you done this to us? We have been so worried about you." His answer equally astounded them when he replied, "Don't you know that I must be about my Father's business?"

Now Joseph thought it was time to take matters into his own hands. "Young man," he said, "I think it is time for you to learn a trade." So Jesus was apprenticed to Joseph as a carpenter. And he became a good carpenter, as it is a noble occupation.

Along with his training as a carpenter, he received, as the son of devout Jewish parents, a thorough education in the traditional Hebrew knowledge of the law and the prophets. This became evident later when in the synagogue in Nazareth he unrolled the sacred scroll to a passage from Isaiah and read, "Surely God is in you and there is no other God." Then he rolled back the scroll and pronounced: "On this day has this prophecy been fulfilled in your midst."

One thing to remember about this part of the world that Jesus was born into is that it is the breeding ground for hatreds—hatreds that run deep and compound with the passage of time.

Antiochus IV, who ruled Syria from 175 to 163 B.C. was devoted to Greek culture and determined to stamp out the Jewish religion. By treachery, he conquered Jerusalem, ravaged the temple, and mur-

Christ Working in the Carpenter Shop, by the author.

The Moment of Decision, Nazareth (egg tempera painting by the author).

dered and crucified over ten thousand of the inhabitants, according to Flavius Josephus, "Antiquities of the Jews."

Later, Mattalhias, a priest, led a revolt against him. His son, Judas Maccabeus, also fought the Jews who had cooperated with Antiochus. In an attempt to restore law and order, the Jews actually requested that the Roman legions intervene. This they did by sentencing the revolters they captured to crucifixion, the standard form of capital punishment.

Jesus, being a carpenter, was, we assume, forced to make crosses for the Roman legions.

He hated this job that he was forced into, as it made him feel as if he was an accessory to a crime. He knew this cruelty was against his Father's will. When, along the roadside north of Nazareth, the agonizing moans of hundreds of these unfortunate victims hanging on crosses filled the air, Jesus could take no more. It was then that he came to his "moment of decision."

As he left the carpenter shop, he again heard the call, "My Son, the time has come for you to go about my business."

And so Jesus wandered off, not knowing where his way led. But, things do not just happen, and he was led by the Spirit to the region of the Jordan where his cousin John was also in revolt against the cruelty of wicked men. John, who had spent many years living with the brotherhood of celibate Jews known as the Essenes, was now performing the cleansing ritual of baptism in the Jordan, and was crying out as a voice in the wilderness to those who suffered from guilty consciences.

Jesus, still suffering from the memories of his last days in the carpenter shop, greeted his cousin, told him of the problems that haunted him day and night, and asked John for help.

"Help from me?" John said. "God forbid. I am not worthy to unlatch your sandals" (as the Scriptures tell us).

But Jesus insisted. So John baptized him and a strange thing happened. Jesus heard a voice. "You are my son in whom I am well pleased. I need your help to do great things for my people on earth. Let me lead you to the solitude of the wilderness."

So it was that in this lonely place where, in a trancelike state for lack of food, he learned to know his Father's will.

He learned things about his Father that would not be revealed for centuries.

God told him things new and enlightening to his thinking. He told him:

I am supreme intelligence.
I am supreme energy.
I am supreme love.

He also said to his Son:

I have planted the seeds of divinity within you;
slowly they will germinate and spring to life and blossom.
The fruit will ripen and be delicious.
He who eats it will taste the energy that nourishes all living things,
and you yourself will become divine and never die.

He said: "You cannot comprehend me in a mere forty days, but I am giving you great power—so much power you will be tempted to abuse it. But you will have enough power to turn your back on temptation. You will have power over all the forces of evil that humans are subject to. But still you will have to suffer at the hands of evil men who will plot to kill you, and will, in the end, succeed. But, as a loving son, you will not disobey me, for in the end, I am giving you a greater reward than all the satanic forces in the universe can offer. I will make you the Light of the World for all eternity."

And God said: "I am giving you three of the world's most precious gifts. I am already sharing with you my 'Supreme Intelligence,' and you are to tell all mankind that through me you are bringing them abundance of life and teaching them to fear not—to be of good cheer.

"Then, with the 'Supreme Energy' I have given

you, you will be able to perform such miraculous acts of physical and mental healing that mankind will recognize my divinity in you.

"Finally, my 'Supreme Love' will, through you, let men see the beauty of the universe I have created when you point to the lilies of the field and tell them that 'Solomon in all his glory was not arrayed like one of these.'

"In this way you will show my great concern for my children on earth by freeing them from the things that darken their lives so that they can better praise and glorify me and know, with assurance, that my love enfolds them."

Jesus performed his mission well. He healed the sick, gave sight to the blind, cleansed the lepers, drove the money-changers from the temple, and accused them of being hypocrites and blind leaders of the blind. He knew his Father's will. Never did he turn away from what he knew was his destiny.

In the end it took a Judas to betray him and an angry mob to convict him.

In the garden, in his agony, he pleaded with his Father for mercy, for from his days as a carpenter, he remembered the agony of crucifixion.

He was crucified, and the veil of the temple was rent from top to bottom, thus ushering in the coming of the Christian age.

Centuries come and go, and slowly, with each new century, God reveals a bit more of himself.

Slowly we learn the lessons Jesus taught:

"The Father and I are one. No man comes to the Father except through me."

And—"I am the resurrection and the life. He that believeth in me shall never die but have eternal life."

I am of the opinion that resurrection and reincarnation are merely two ways of saying the same thing. A daffodil comes back each year as a daffodil, and each spring we eagerly wait for its return. And as Nietzsche says: "My doctrine is: live so that thou mayest desire to live again. That is thy duty. For in any case thou wilt again. . . . "

And as Voltaire says: "It is not more surprising to be born twice than once. Everything in nature is resurrection."

And to quote Walt Whitman: "I know that I am deathless. No doubt I have died myself ten thousand times before. I laugh at what you call dissolution, and I know the amplitude of time."

Kahlil Gibran: "Know, therefore, that from the greater silence I shall return. . . . Forget not that I shall come back to you . . a little while, a moment of rest upon the wind, and another woman shall bear me."

Again, Mohandas Gandhi said: "Believing as I do in the theory of rebirth, I live in the hope that if not in this birth, in some other birth I shall be able to hug all humanity in friendly embrace."

Albert Schweitzer writes: "The idea of reincarnation contains a most comforting explanation of reality by means of which Indian thought surmounts difficulties which baffle the thinkers of Europe."

And going back to 325 A.D. when at the Council of Nicaea the "Apostles' Creed" was adopted as doctrine by the new Christian church, we read: "I believe in the Holy Ghost, the holy Christian church, the forgiveness of sins, *the resurrection of the body*, and life everlasting."

How one believes is a matter of personal choice. Many of the world's great minds have pondered deeply about resurrection and reincarnation and expressed their opinions, and many, without giving much thought to the subject, have expressed their opinions with a blunt, "I don't believe it."

Based on a long life that, I am convinced, has been led and guided by a powerful outside "Source" or "Force"—whatever you want to call it—I choose to join ranks with those whose personal opinions were previously quoted on the subject. In fact, despite many of the reversals of fortune all human creatures are subject to, I would consider a repeat performance a great privilege.

Throughout this book I have written other poems under the heading: "And God said."

"And God said,
I have given you a
great gift.
I have given you the ability to
think.
Do not let anything interfere
with the use of this gift,
neither prejudice, nor intolerance,
nor bigotry, nor politics, nor
religious doctrine.
For if you do, you will
enslave yourself to the past.
Treasure an open mind
that you may make the best use
of this gift from your Creator.
Take time to THINK.

In the world at large, belief in reincarnation has, in general, been far in advance of America. However, this is changing. On December 18, 1994, in *USA Today* a Gallup poll reported that in the United States, twenty-seven percent of adults believe in reincarnation, whereas in 1990 only twenty-one percent shared this belief. This trend shows there should be great progress in the twenty-first century.

It is not our quantum mechanical body that will be resurrected. That, like everything in nature, has its time. A human being is made up of body, mind, and soul. Through the slow process of evolution, we are learning more about the body and the mind, and in the twenty-first century, a great deal more will doubtless be revealed to us.

Since the scientific minds of the twenty-first century will doubtless be intent on solving the riddles of the universe, we can rest assured that the mystery of the human soul will be subjected to close scrutiny.

So, within the field of human understanding, let us just say that the soul—that indestructible part of you—is our link with eternity. And that the soul is what will be reincarnated into another body, at another time, just as the soul of the Father became incarnate in the Son.

As Jesus discovered when he went into the wilderness, there is no better place where, as Plato said: "Thinking is the talking of the soul with itself."

The fast pace of big-city life does not leave room for the quiet contemplation necessary for the maturing and development of the human soul. As we find in the following poem from *Residue*, only in **solitude** can one make contact with God.

Oh, solitude, thou precious thing
That brings us nearer to the heart of God,
That lets us breathe the freshness of the sod in
    spring,
The tender notes of birds upon the wing,
Laughing waves upon the shore,
These things our souls have need of more
Than all the struggle and the strife
And hardened ways of city life.
For, after all, should life be spent
Upon some fleeting pleasure bent,
That like a fancy elfin dream
Or some far-fetched and hopeless scheme
Be torn from us to leave but dross
As poor remembrances of our loss?
Then let my narrow vision range
Beyond this world that's ever strange.
Give me a calmly balanced mood
That seals my fate in solitude.

Webster defines the soul as "The principles of life, feeling, thought, and action in man, regarded as a distinct entity separate from the body, and commonly held to be separable in existence from the body; the spiritual part of man as distinct from the physical."

As one makes a conscious effort to exercise the soul, one will find that it is gathering new strength that one never realized existed. The beauty that radiates from all of nature that surrounds one will add new excitement to life. When one discovers the close relationship between Self and Spirit, the joy of living will take on new meaning. (Again from *Residue*):

> Would you grow strong?
> Then gather strength
> Where there is beauty found,
> For ugliness is weariness
> That preys upon the soul.
> The plant that lifts
> Ten times its weight;
> Witchhazel bloom
> Upon a frosty autumn morn;
> The bursting of pink buds
> When blossoms are born;
> These all have strength
> Untested yet by man.
>
> Would you grow strong?
> Then take a lengthy draught
> Of loveliness
> And you will find
> That nature never wastes a thing.

We are encouraged by the possibility of taking a great step forward toward a higher and more disciplined level of existence where thought and action are guided by a power that comes from a universal constructive principle embodied in each of us.

The late Rev. Dr. Norman Vincent Peale has written many books that focus on the latent potential in every human being. This discovery he made within himself was what inspired the Rev. Dr. Robert Schuller, pastor of the Crystal Cathedral in Garden Grove, California. Schuller, through his preaching, is now passing it on to millions who listen every Sunday morning as his radio and television programs encircle the globe.

This positive way of thinking emphatically points out the vast differences between those who overcome and those who succumb. And to dramatize the points in his sermon, he often brings in witnesses as examples of those who have overcome handicaps. Some have struggled to overcome poverty, and some have conquered mental and physical limitations.

The Creator has built into every human being a "Potential Factor" as part of his or her personality. This is one of the powerful forces, with quantum limits, that is our responsibility to discover within ourselves. This is what Dr. Schuller has written about in one of his late books entitled, *If It's Going to Be, It's Up to Me*. This is a message that is doing so much to raise the dignity of African Americans with the battle cry of Martin Luther King: "We shall overcome."

When I was an active ten-year-old youngster, I was suddenly knocked down by polio. When the doctor solemnly led my father and mother into our library and announced, "Don't expect him to ever walk again," Dad replied, "That lad is going to walk again if it's the last thing he does."

Dad was a real "overcomer," not a "succumber." It was then that he started on a program of "tough love." He instinctively began giving me all of the same treatments for which Sister Kenney later became famous.

Quite naturally, my mother was overcome with sympathy, but Dad knew that sympathy could only be damaging. As he told her, "He is going to have to grow up like everybody else. He had a bad strike against him. So he's got to be tough, as he'll be here long after we're gone and he will have to get along on his own."

So, it was then, that plans were made for my mother to take me to the Maclean Sanatorium in St. Louis. This was the leading place in the country, at the time, for the treatment of polio patients. And there, after six months of strenuous exercise treatments, operations and braces, I was able to be back on my feet.

Normally, post-polio syndrome sets in somewhere between thirty and forty years after the inception of the disease, but I have avoided it for many years by a daily program of systematic exercise.

Some years ago, I asked a woman who had had polio if she did any exercising. "Oh," she said, "I'm too old for that." She had become a "succumber." If you think you're handicapped, you are.

Dr. Schuller's broadcast, "The Hour of Power," has contributed to raising the dignity level of human beings. Negative views about sin, taught for centuries, have only stunted the growth of our self-esteem. We know we have been created by a loving God, one who teaches us to harbor positive thoughts. We can use this "power of positive thinking" to help us change the course of our direction when needed.

This next great step in the same direction should bring us to a higher level in our quest.

On August 21, 1996, I wrote another "And God Said:"

Please explain to me, O God,

      Who you are.
      What you are.
      Why you are.
      Where you are.
These are questions that puzzle me.
Please explain to me the
mysteries of your universe.
Tell me what I should know
that on my walk through life
I do not trip on
unseen stones
for lack of light to see my way.
And God said:
    I was before the world began.
    I made your yesterday.
    I am making your today
    and, I will make your tomorrow.
    I will always be.
And God said:
    I am supreme intelligence.
    I made you to be a part of
    my quantum universe.
    I made you in my image
    with a soul that, like me,
    will never die
    so you may know eternity.
And God said:

I am proud of what I do.
I created you in my image
so, please
do not break the mirror.
The glass might cut you.
But, as I am proud of myself
and what I do,
you must do the things you
can be proud of.
And God said:
You cannot see me
but yet, you can see me
for I am everywhere
and in everything
from the smallest to the largest.
You see me in everything
that is beautiful,
for out of my great love
for you,
I knew it would give you pleasure.'
And so God answered my questions
by explaining himself.
And the answers satisfied me,
for they made me rich
beyond riches.
For now I know that
he is part of me,
and I am part of him
and all things are one.

Ralph Waldo Emerson, clergyman and poet (born 1803), was an independent thinker who championed the divine potential latent in every human being. He saw that just as God was incarnate in the Christ, so God incarnates himself in all humans.

Again, in the year A.D. 325 at the Council at Nicea, a new mystery was added to the teaching of the early Christian Church by the invention of the Trinity, an attempt to define the attributes of our Supreme Being. However, in the coming twenty-first century, thinkers, who in an unending search for new knowledge, are subjecting everything, including the Trinity, to close scrutiny and analysis, would rather define the attributes of Supreme Being in a way that everyone can readily understand. I would suggest:

Supreme Intelligence
Supreme Energy
Supreme Love.

Since we now see God as "Supreme Intelligence," "Supreme Energy," and "Supreme Love," and, as the Bible informs us that we are created in God's image, we can conclude that God is within us. We need to express our divinity by showing love to one another. We bear a responsibility for all our actions.

Now, as we are about to enter this new twenty-first century, it is for us to learn more of what Christ learned while he was alone with his Father in the wilderness in order that we may become more Christlike. This will be a good exercise for the soul.

Supreme Intelligence

Although research about the structure and functioning of the human body is being carried on in laboratories around the world, it is impossible to comprehend a SUPREME INTELLIGENCE capable of creating a machine as complicated as the mechanical human body. It is made up of billions of cells. Each cell has its own intelligence and is capable of reacting in harmony with its neighbor cell. For example, a stomach cell knows exactly when to initiate the digestive process and how many hormones are needed to metabolize a molecule of sugar to convert it into energy.

Likewise, it is impossible to understand a SUPREME INTELLIGENCE capable of creating a nervous system with its billions of neuron connectors that can involuntarily and automatically control every action from creative thought to total recall. This cell intelligence has for its source the SUPREME INTELLIGENCE that motivates every action in the entire universe.

Perhaps this is what Albert Einstein meant when he said, "I want to know God's thoughts—the rest is details."

The "details" leave us, as I'm sure they left Einstein, in a quandary. But at least he tried. And we as amateur scientists must not give up in our quest for an understanding of "SUPREME INTELLIGENCE."

In the beginning of the twentieth century, Einstein made public his "Quantum Theory." Physicists in general now acknowledge that at the deepest level of the natural world, we find the quantum field. A "quantum" can be simply defined as the smallest unit of electricity, light, or other form of energy that can possibly exist. These are the all-powerful forces that hold the universe together. Scientific discoveries in the field of quantum reality have given us X rays, radars, masers, lasers, transistors, solidstate electrons, superconductors, antibiotics, and genetic engineering, and have made it possible to explore deeper into the mystery of creation. All of this, as I have mentioned, has come about through the process of evolution, which is God in action as He expands the scope of the human mind.

Supreme Energy

We know that all forms of energy in the universe are transmitted in the form of vibrations. Science has developed numerous ways to measure these vibrations in ways that can furnish us with useful information. For practical purposes, we can classify these vibrations into three categories: LUMINIFEROUS, CALORIFIC, and ACTIONOID. For humans, it is important to understand these energy vibrations that surround us, and to fine-tune our minds to receive them, just as the strings of a piano are fine-tuned to the sound vibration when a tuning fork is struck.

First, let us consider the LUMINIFEROUS RAYS: These are the vibrations of light from our Source—the sun. These rays can be seen but not felt—at least, they are not meant to be felt. But they are powerful enough to give you a bad sunburn and might eventually lead to skin cancer.

Next, let us consider the CALORIFIC RAYS: These also emanate from our Source—the sun. (Source is the term used by the ancient order of the Druids for Supreme Being.) These are the vibrations that can be felt but not seen. Every living creature has its own way of protecting itself from too much heat or cold. Birds are equipped with insulating feathers and animals with insulating fur. People have had to invent their own ways of protecting themselves from the extremes of heat and cold.

Thirdly, let us consider the ACTIONOID RAYS: These are also mysterious vibrations from our Source—the sun. These vibrations can neither be felt nor seen. Because of their quantum character, they cannot be measured. But they can, without any visible effort, crack the hardest seed and bring forth life in all its beauty. This is the mysterious Actionoid force that makes all life on this planet an integral part of the universe. This is the mysterious quantum field that surrounds every living thing in the cosmos. **This is the power that furnishes the electricity that keeps the heart pumping twenty-four hours a day for a lifetime.**

For a person fortunate enough to be an artist or a poet, the wonders of nature that surround us can be the tuning fork that keeps one sensitive to the vibrating forces that surround us. And, when raised to the highest level, marvelous things can happen. One can feel the genius radiating from the music by Mozart and the beauty of the Sistine Chapel when Michelangelo touched the hand of God.

And so—(again from *Residue*):

Let the beauty of thy nature, Lord
now be revealed through me,
that man may see thy loveliness
and praises sing to thee.

The force of Supreme Energy has no limits.

Who knows the heart in a poet's breast
where a thousand wild forces
are seldom at rest.
His tempo is set by the waves on the shore.
The spirit of music he feels in the roar
of winds from the north.
No peace do they bring
until he bridles their rhyme
to the songs he would sing.
Moonbeams reflecting celestial light
make lovely the magical realm of the night.
The perfume of flowers;
the song of a bird;
these rare gifts of God
in his verses are heard.
Fiercer than lightning that shatters the sky,
deeper than pain—higher than joy,
these rage in a fight only death can destroy
in the heart and the soul
of a poet.

Supreme Love

One of the first things a child learns in Sunday school is that God is love. We can hope, as we take a next step into the twenty-first century, that we learn the meaning of God as SUPREME LOVE.

Since evolution is God in action, this next step can lead to a fuller spiritual life experience. The Holy Bible is the greatest love story ever written. The many authors who have shared in its writing have been inspired by personal experiences and visions. From the letters of Saint Paul and the gospels, the Latin Vulgate written by Jerome near the end of the fourth century, through the various English translations and revisions, it has continued to head the best-seller list in the entire world.

If you were going to write on the subject of love, just one look at the many aspects of love in any Bible concordance would stagger the mind.

However, a good starting point would be 1 Corinthians 13 written by Saint Paul:

> Though I speak with the tongues of men and angels, and have not love, I have become as sounding brass or clanging cymbals. And though I have the gift of prophecy and understand all mysteries and all knowledge, and though I have all faith so that I could move mountains, and have not love, I have nothing. And though I bestow all my goods to feed the poor,

and though I give my body to be burned, but have not love, it profits me nothing.

Love suffers long and is kind; love does not envy; love does not parade itself, is not puffed up; does not behave rudely; does not seek its own, is not provoked, thinks no evil, does not rejoice in iniquity but rejoices in the truth; bears all things, believes all things, hopes all things, endures all things, love never fails. But where there are prophecies, they shall fail; where there are tongues, they shall cease; where there is knowledge, it will vanish away. For we know in part and we prophesy in part. But when that which is perfect has come, then that which is in part will be done away.

When I was a child, I spoke as a child, I thought as a child, I understood as a child, but when I became a man, I put away childish things. For now we see in a mirror dimly, but then face to face. Now I know in part, but then I shall know just as I am known.

And now abide faith, hope, love, these three; but the greatest of these is love.

The mystery of love is that the more one gives the more one keeps. It is the flowing form of energy that, in a mysterious way, surrounds every living thing.

Love, as one of the most powerful forces in the universe, requires great care in handling. Managed properly, it can be one of the greatest blessings humans can experience. With mismanagement, there is no limit to its destructive power. It takes constant practice to cultivate love's great potential that can be available to everyone.

As a thinking human being, one has been given the ability to make choices that will affect one's married life, one's friendships, and one's business relationships. One can choose love, consideration, trust, compassion, sympathy. These are all positive emotions that will make each day, no matter how busy, a real joy.

Or, one is likewise free to choose the negative emotions. Unfortunately, many people do not make a choice. The negative emotions choose them and they succumb to all sorts of devastating forces, such as anger, distrust, envy, greed, and selfishness—all of which lead to anxiety, guilt, and sorrow.

Since feelings are all abstract, the choosing of positive emotions makes it possible to live in a creative atmosphere that will lead to revelation, insight, discovery, invention, intuition, and peace of mind. The choosing of negative emotions limits the world, whereas positive emotions expand the world.

One must never forget that one is a thinking human being, and as such, has been given a free will to choose between good and evil. Again as I have written, "You are an Instrument":

> You are God's instrument
> on which you can play
> a hymn of praise,
> a rhapsody in times of joy,
> a lullaby to a sleepy child,
> a love song on your wedding day,
> a lament when you lose a friend.
> You are God's instrument
> when you are in tune with
> the harmony of the universe.

The combining of these three mighty forces—Supreme Intelligence, Supreme Energy, and Supreme Love—forms the mightiest force of all—the force of Creativity. This is the force that makes everything in the universe possible. Creativity is a quantum evolutionary force that is continually shaping and reshaping humans on a slow, but sure, upward path.

In addition, the Creator has furnished us with an unending supply of mysteries. Without mystery there would be no challenges and no progress. Without curious minds willing to attack the so-called unsolvable mysteries, civilization would probably be back in the Stone Age. We have to admire the great minds that have brought us up to the present level. And what is encouraging is the number of brilliant young scientists meeting the challenges of the future.

Faith

On the subject of "faith," it is important to start with a positive mind-set. Without a strong self-confident faith, no scientific accomplishment can be achieved. Start with the fixed belief that what you thoroughly believe will actually happen.

Faith is one of the most powerful forces of energy and one that Christ used so effectively during his short ministry on earth.

Although religion has attempted to teach faith for centuries, it is, because of its quantum character, something that cannot be taught. It is possible, however, to teach the proper handling of it as a strong force in our lives.

We know, for example, what a powerful force electricity is when handled properly, and how dangerous it can be when mishandled. We also know that faith, like medicine, when taken according to directions, can cure an illness. But faith, like a medicine, should carry a label to warn against the consequence of misuse.

In the "Foreword," I referred to the soul as a compass that silently, but surely, shows one a course for one's journey on earth.

As one travels along life's pathway, one can be compared to a captain of a ship or the pilot of an airplane. When setting out on a journey, it is essential to have a goal and to chart a course. By the time one has ended the journey, one may have modified the course, modified or even abandoned the original goal for a new goal. But during the journey, one has been gaining new insight and understandings, shaping new thoughts. For in life, you see, the goal, the focus, the direction is essential, even though the goal may not always be accomplished. Not having a goal is worse than not reaching it.

In the early days of sailing ships, the skipper set his course by the compass. It was very important that the compass be accurate if he were to trust it. Establishing the accuracy was known as compensating the compass. The magnetized needle of the compass is attracted by the magnetic field of the earth that points it to the north magnetic pole. The compass card (referred to by sailors as the "compass rose") is then adjusted to the direction that the needle points.

In this advanced scientific age, the compass, along with new high tech instruments, can, by contacting satellites, indicate the positions of ships at sea with great accuracy.

Thus, the soul can be compared to a compass that directs one's course through life. But, like a nautical compass, it needs adjustment to accurately keep us on a true course.

Most everyone has had the experience at one time or another of being led in some direc-

tion he had not planned, or of doing something he had not intended to do. And often, in retrospect, he realizes he seemed to have been directed by an outside force. These can be the faith-building experiences that add drama to life and make it exciting.

Writing this book has been just such an experience. It has, from beginning to end, been directed by an outside force—a force that, in the quantum universe, is beyond my understanding. However, just knowing that it does exist, is what faith is all about.

A strong faith in the positive can work miracles. Norman Cousins made a profound statement some years ago based on personal experience. "Belief creates biology." And a strong faith has the ability to heal.

Christ often criticized his disciples when he would say, "Oh, ye of little faith." He knew that without faith there could be no miracle.

Faith, being a quantum commodity, cannot be taught, bought, or sold. It will slowly evolve based on our awareness.

We had dear friends, who, at a critical point in their lives, decided to build a chapel on their estate after having seen one at the Folk Museum at Lillehammer in Norway. They spent nine busy years building the chapel during a time of great personal stress, when four of their children were involved in the Second World War. When it was finished, they published a book, *Faith Builds a Chapel*.

At the end of the book they pointed out a discovery that they had made about themselves. *Not only were they building a chapel—the chapel was building them.*

As we go into the next exciting century, let us slowly but surely cultivate the ability to make use of this wonderful source of energy. Let us use it to develop a stronger and more flexible faith so we can enjoy its wonder-working power.

Growth is synonymous with life. Keep dreaming and you keep growing. Faith is never completed or fulfilled. Your faith has unlimited potential. If you say you have lost faith, it means that you have given up on your dreams—you have turned off your "Source" of energy, and it's time to turn it back on again.

Prayer

Prayer is another of life's mighty forces that, like love and faith, requires thoughtful care. To begin, the Lord's Prayer that Christ taught his followers, should serve as a model and should not be repeated parrot-like, as is so often the case.

When everything is going well, one may have the feeling that one is in complete control and in no need of any divine guidance. Just a word of warning! This is the danger point when things could go wrong. This is the time to start forming the habit of daily prayer just to be thankful for all of one's good fortune. One will find that it has the therapeutic effect of supporting one in times of stress and need.

Now, what about the times when everything does go wrong? What about the times when all hope seems to be lost? These are the times when the normal human reaction is to cry out to the Creator for help. How one's prayers will be answered will not depend on what one wants, but on how the all-knowing Supreme Being chooses to answer.

At some unexpected time in life, everyone goes through an experience like the one I had some years ago: For over ten years my wife had suffered from an ailment that became progressively worse. Finally it became apparent that an operation was the only choice left. Three days after the operation was performed, she died. Needless to say, I did more praying in those three days than I had ever done in my life; praying that I could bring her home where she could make a complete recovery.

Now what was I to believe? I had always understood that God answers prayer, so where was he when I needed him? Why had my faith been so badly shattered?

Now, years later in retrospect, I realize my prayers were answered. What I had been doing was selfishly praying for what I wanted, and not for her welfare. She had suffered enough to make her death a welcome release, and who was I to contradict the will of God?

Mortals often make the mistake I made. This is where one might, in anger, conclude that there is no God. This is where, if faith lacks strength, it could be wrecked. This is when one needs to learn the lesson Christ taught when in the Garden of Gethsemane, on his last night as a mortal on this earth, he spent many agonizing hours praying to his Father that the cup of death should be removed. Finally, he bravely submitted to his fate with the words, "Nevertheless, not my will, but thine be done." Thus he taught us that we must all submit to the Power that put us on this earth in the first place.

In this way we learn that, while the laws we humans make can be broken, the laws the Creator makes cannot be broken. That is everything and all one needs to know. God is our best friend. Keep up the friendship. Take time to pray daily. From time to time check the connection. There may be something that he wants us to do to fulfill the reason for our being here.

I had just finished reading to a friend what I had written about prayer when he surprised me. He took his wallet from his pocket and read "Prayer for Protection" that he had cherished for years. As a spiritual gift, he would like to share it with you.

Prayer for Protection

Night and day, never ceasing for a single moment, the prayers of Silent Unity go out for you.

Should you need help, wherever you are, whatever the hour of day or night, let but an unspoken cry rise from your heart, and with the speed of Spirit the prayers of Silent Unity will be with you.

Prayer is a protecting power. It unifies you instantly with God, whose love is your protection.

The light of God surrounds me;
The love of God enfolds me;
The power of God protects me;
The presence of God watches over me;
Wherever I am, God is!

Mother Teresa

When the average person thinks of Mother Teresa, it is only natural to visualize her as a person highly motivated spiritually. Worldwide, she is revered for the helpful dedication she showed to the poor, the suffering, and those who have lost hope.

However, few think of her as a shrewd businesswoman heading a large organization known as the Sisters of Charity. And, during her lifetime, as a businesswoman, she handed out thousands of small red business cards that quote her credo:

>*The fruit of silence is*
>PRAYER.
>*The fruit of prayer is*
>FAITH.
>*The fruit of faith is*
>LOVE.
>*The fruit of love is*
>SERVICE.
>*The fruit of service is*
>PEACE.

Prayer for the 21st Century

Our heavenly Father,
You, who with
   Supreme intelligence
   Supreme energy, and
   Supreme love,
Created this beautiful universe,
We thank you
   For honoring us by making us
   A part of your creation.
We thank you for creating the Christ
   Who sacrificed his life to become
The light of the world.
Do not permit us to pray for what we
   Think are our needs or wants,
But pray only that your will be done,
Trusting that then
We will be richly blessed.

Conclusion

There is no need to give any of the following suggestions a priority as they are all important:

EDUCATION: When we have completed our formal education as young people, that is only the beginning. Our high school or college diploma should not point out our accomplishments, but should rather read, "THIS MARKS THE BEGINNING OF A LIFELONG GROWTH PROCESS OF OUR OWN MAKING"—one that should be pursued with enthusiasm.

DISCIPLINE: This is something that should begin in the form of parental guidance at a very early age in order for it to become ingrained in a child's mind in such a way that it will shape his or her personality later on. If it is not started very early, it will be much harder to develop later on in life. There should be no fear of danger that it will warp a child's personality. It will only strengthen it. Any parent who deprives a child of discipline is doing irreparable damage. Without discipline, nothing worthwhile is ever accomplished.

READING: Reading stimulates the mind, and since "You are what you think," keep the level of your reading on a high plane. There are plenty of good books. Don't bother with the trash. Your mind is like a muscle that needs exercise to keep it expanding. Otherwise, like any muscle, it will atrophy.

WORSHIP: If you think one hour a week in church is enough—it isn't. It may help and will certainly improve relations with your fellow humans. However, if you want to develop a more spiritual life, plan to take time for private study and worship. Today there are many fine books available for your inspiration that will stimulate your mind.

Years ago we inherited a custom from some very dear friends. Each morning we have a candle burning on our breakfast table, feeling that any day when we can get up and have reasonably good health, well, that is cause for celebration. God loves a grateful heart.

TELEVISION: Depending on how television is used, it can furnish good entertainment and education, or become a mind-wrecking disturbance. With programs featuring violence and crime, it contributes to the nation's high level of crime.

DIET: At the beginning of the twentieth century, vitamins as a supplement for an unbalanced diet were unknown. The danger of consuming too much fat was also unknown. At that time the quality of beef was judged by how well it was marbleized with fat. However, science is continuing to make discoveries in the field of nutrition that will lead to a much healthier lifestyle.

Dr. Victor Lindlar, for many years director of the Chicago Department of Public Health, wrote a weekly column for the *Chicago Tribune* that always ended with his favorite slogan, "You are what you eat." Just one look around and the truth of this statement is very apparent. Obesity ranks high on the list as one of the killer diseases.

EXERCISE: One of the great achievements of this century is the emphasis on the importance of exercise for people of all ages. At the beginning of the twentieth century it was not stressed, and for women, it was considered not ladylike. Exercise is now considered to be the best way to tap the universal source of energy that will improve the functioning of the body. No matter what your age, find your own best exercise routine and don't break it.

REST: Under ordinary circumstances, seven to nine hours of sleep is considered sufficient. But, if you have been under considerable strain, more is needed to recharge your batteries. Your general physical condition determines how much rest you need. Remember, too much time in bed can be enervating. Unlike machines that run down with too much use, the human body is capable of improving the more it is used. Doctors now get patients out of bed in a hurry during hospitalization, as they know that complete bed rest for only a few weeks will cause as much physical deterioration as experienced by someone who has aged ten years.

SMOKING: At the beginning of the twentieth century, the dangers of smoking were unrecognized. When I was a university student many years ago, I visited a medical science exhibit being held on campus. On display was a section of a cadaver lung from a heavy smoker. It was almost black—a veritable ash pile. I don't know if the poor creature had died of emphysema, cancer, or heart failure. In any case, there are better ways to go. Smoking is a nasty habit. I know, because I found I had to break it. Years ago, in the morning when I would go to the studio to work after breakfast, I would light my pipe. When it went out, I would stoke it up again. The habit finally got such a hold that I knew I would have to break it. I decided the best way would be to condition my mind into believing how bad the pipe tasted. Not long after making the decision, I lit my pipe one morning, and in disgust said to myself, *Gosh, my mouth tastes just like the bottom of a bird cage.* And with that, I put all my pipes and tobacco onto a shelf in the closet and never brought them out again.

ALCOHOL: The use of alcohol in moderation is not

harmful and may indeed be beneficial. In excess, it could be a killer! Alcoholism can ruin a family, lose friends, and turn a speeding car into a deadly weapon.

RETIREMENT: Corporate America has set a time limit to a worker's useful years. This can be a very devastating experience unless looked upon as an opportunity to start a new career. Perhaps there is some new field of endeavor that you have dreamed about that could keep you even more occupied than your past career. Whatever you do, don't let the old rocking chair get you. Ruth and I have adopted the philosophy, "It's better to wear out than rust out." We know from our experience and that of friends that if one doesn't use it, one will lose it.

These are just a few suggestions to help you establish a healthy lifestyle.**Make a conscious effort to realize that the quantum field of the universe that surrounds everyone is charged with all the energy needed to sustain life. The key ingredients of clean air, pure water, and wholesome food are dependent on our wise stewardship on this earth. Humankind needs to treat these as valuable gifts from the Creator, which have been put here for our use and not abuse.**

Now, just a word to welcome you, the reader,

into the twenty-first century that, I believe, will be known as an "age of great miracles." First of all, that you are here, at this time and place, is for you miracle number one. Do not take it for granted. You are here for a special purpose. It is up to you to discover that purpose.

I will now outline five steps that should make it possible for you to lead a longer and more enjoyable life in the twenty-first century. Call it your training program for the future.

1. Step No. 1: Follow the suggestions (beginning on page 69) by fixing your mind on the "Do's" and "Don'ts" listed as they apply to you.
2. Step No. 2: Turn back to the "Foreword" and read, with special emphasis, the remarks by Frank Pechman.
3. Step No. 3: SUPREME INTELLIGENCE (page 50) Read with a view to learning more about your mechanical body. The more you know and understand what you have been given, the better you will be able to give it proper care. If you abuse it, without fail, you will pay the price. If you do give it proper care and repair when needed, you will have a better chance of living a longer and more useful life.
4. Step No. 4: SUPREME ENERGY (page 52) Energy is everything. With dynamic energy and enthusiasm, anything is possible. Without energy

you can do nothing. Train yourself to become conscious of the **field of energy that surrounds you.** It is the Creator's gift to you for your entire life.
5. Step No. 5: SUPREME LOVE (page 55) This is another great gift from your Creator. You will enrich your own life by giving generously to others. You will find that the more you give, the more you will get back.

By following this simple self-training program, you will enrich whatever religious affiliations you now have—or do not have. There is more evil in the world than one can absorb; so, if you just shut it out, you can easily find enough GOOD to make yourself truly happy.

With the outpouring of new discoveries in the many fields of science, miraculous events will occur and many mysteries will be solved.

As we evolve into a higher state in the scheme of creation, **Christ will take on a new and fuller dimension than ever before.** As science advances, an outpouring of new discoveries and miraculous events will occur; today's mysteries will have solutions tomorrow.

Know that your spirit is the real you. Your soul is the road map that will guide you to become the spiritual creature that your Creator meant you to be.

How humankind makes use of the scientific discoveries that the next century will be capable of furnishing is yet to be seen. We cannot forget that for centuries technology has been used for destructive ends, which have been consciously chosen by those wedded to death rather than life.

However, there are the idealists and dreamers on the other side, dedicated to morality and the promotion of life, love, and creativity, and making this world a fit habitation for humans.

The most important discovery will come when men and women become truly conscious of the fact that the spirit is the real you. It is your soul that will guide you to becoming the spiritual creature that your Creator meant you to be.

Your Creator has honored you by giving you a short visit to this beautiful planet. You are progressing, through a process of metamorphosis, from immortality to mortality and back to immortality. How long you will be here is not for you to know. Strive to make the best use of each day. Keep in mind that it is in the here and now that each one of us should be formulating plans for our next life on earth. Without fear, we can then return to eternity—our home—with the comforting feeling that we have used our God-given talents to the fullest.

Bibliography

A good friend, Dr. Roberta Nauman, who, with a critical eye, went over my manuscript, suggested I supply a bibliography, as some readers, with an equally critical eye, might want to know the source of my information. Since she made the suggestion, I have been trying to find an excuse to get out of the job.

Each morning I begin my day with an exercise routine. A part of it consists of sitting on the desk in my studio with five-pound weights strapped to my ankles and kicking for half an hour. Out the front window, I have a wonderful view overlooking a bay and the far landscape. The beauty of the small world that surrounds me is breathtaking.

However, my mind is not encapsulated in either time or space. The *Sources* of much that I have written come from *Out There* and cannot be found in any bibliography. This is especially true of the poetry. Where necessary, references can be found with the text.

When I say that the *Source* of much that I have written came from *Out There*, I am referring to that part of the quantum field where the primordial field exists and can be detected only when the mind is quiet and in tune with the wonders of the universe. In this quantum field of energy, *Out There*, is to be found all the creative forces that have so abundantly enriched mankind.

So—there goes the bibliography.

It has been suggested that I list some of the sources of information that readers might find helpful and interesting. However, a word of caution: unless they are read, they will have no effect.

Here is the list:

1. The Holy Bible. I am acquainted with the King James Version, the Standard Revised Version, the Scofield Version. Up to this point I find the Positive Thinkers Version the most helpful because of the explanations that accompany each book.

    An elderly pastor once told me that the Bible can be compared to a beautiful garden in which one can walk and admire the works of the Creator. But, turn a pig loose in it and it will soon become a slimy mire.
2. *Putting Your Faith into Action Today,* by Dr. Robert Schuller. This is an excellent small text for daily reading.
3. *If It's Going to Be, It's Up to Me,* by Dr. Robert Schuller. This is a dynamic stimulant to put one on the positive thinking track.
4. *Perfect Health,* by Deepak Chopra. Published by Harmony Books. A worldwide best-seller.
5. *Ageless Body, Timeless Mind,* by Deepak Chopra.

Published by Harmony Books. Another bestseller that everyone should read.
6. *Seven Spiritual Laws of Success,* by Deepak Chopra. Published by Amber Allen Publishing.
7. *Rescuing the Bible from the Fundamentalists,* by Bishop John Shelby Spong. Published by Harper's, San Francisco.
8. *Why Christianity Must Change or Die,* by Bishop John Shelby Spong. This is of timely importance.
9. *The Five Equations that Changed the World,* by Michael Guillen, Ph.D. This is an important book by a noted Harvard mathematician, emphasizing the power and poetry of mathematics.
10. *Visions*, by Michio Kaku. Published by Anchor Books. Gives an idea of how science will revolutionize the 21st Century.

Now, just an author's final comment:

My wife, Ruth, and I have discovered that a spiritual life can be rewarding and comforting when it becomes a QUEST. **However, it requires time and effort.** As I have pointed out on page 70 under the title WORSHIP, one hour a week in church is not enough to do more than greet friends. In fact, spirituality is not found in any church, synagogue, or mosque. However, when we make of religion a QUEST, it can produce rich rewards by giving us a deeper appreciation of all the natural wonders in the universe that surround us, and, in doing so, provide a better understanding of our Creator as SUPREME INTELLIGENCE, SUPREME ENERGY, and SUPREME LOVE.